Midlife Calculus

Midlife Calculus

Britt Kaufmann

poems by

Britt Kaufmann

Press 53
Winston-Salem

Press 53, LLC
PO Box 30314
Winston-Salem, NC 27130

First Edition

THE PRESS 53 IMMERSION SERIES
EDITED BY CHRISTOPHER FORREST

Cover image by Martin de Arriba
licensed for free use through Pexels

Author photo by Cheyenne Dancy
facebook.com/CheyenneDancyPhotography

Cover design by Britt Kaufmann

Library of Congress Control Number
2024940586

ISBN 978-1-950413-82-9

*Dedicated to the Math Department
at Mountain Heritage High School*

Acknowledgments

The author thanks the editors of the publications where these poems first appeared, occasionally in different form:

BRILLIG: A Micro Lit Mag, "Dementia Sandwich," "Enrolled," and "If things feel unfair, count."

Cosmic Daffodil, "Same"

Heimat Review, "Yoga for the Apathy of Rocks"

Hog River Press "No One Really Understands Gravity"

J Journal: New Writing on Justice, "He Leaves Instructions on the Whiteboard: Systems of Linear Inequalities"

Kakalak, "Rights County Appalachia"

Math Values, "Bucket List," and "Domain"

Mathematical Association of America: FOCUS, "Z-Score of Zero"

Pine Mountain Sand & Gravel Contemporary Appalachian Writing, "Property Management"

Poetry in Plain Sight, North Carolina Poetry Society, "Mathematics of Change"

Redheaded Stepchild, "Coastal Prayer"

Scientific American, "Midlife Calculus"

Contents

Midlife Calculus

Enrolled

If I take calculus,
   the study of how things change,
Could I learn to love it,
   the curve of my menopausal belly?
Come to terms with the exponential functions
   that reflect from the corners of my eyes?
Appreciate waves,
   as though fanned embers danced murmurations over my torso?

Sign me up.
It is all self-inflicted.

Why so few poems lately?

Lord, but
   if I pay attention,
   really pay attention,
   it all reduces down to
   common names for misery—

a swooping songbird hit by a car
   not even the crows will pick,
a receding hairline,
a pending eviction,
an invisible cat hair on the inside of my mask.

Coinciding [Plot] Lines

We long to be the hero of the story, though
the fiction is what we imagine:
time suspended in fairytale futures—
snowglobe epilogs of existence.

The bulk of the book is, inevitably,
    rigorous study,
    an accumulation of bullies,
    mean teachers, mentors,
    the labored acquisition of fickle friends,
    grueling tests and trials
    in escalating disasters.

If we could we would
detour to the denouement,
simplify, constantly choose
the quietude of being a foil.

Coastal Prayer

In the pre-dawn glow, the pelican aunties
look down on me from their pier posts in sleepy disapproval,
their eyes set in *Dia de los Muertos* faces
as I paddleboard the calm intracoastal
before the boats wake.

No, not me, out to sea, among the crashing waves,
yet still in waters beyond my depth on tremulous footing
where little fishes leap like dashes on a slope field,
the beauty of their tiny splashes mar the surface and make light
a terror flight from a predatory snapper.

Give me a rule to follow:
    The constant rule through all these changes,
    The power rule to not give in,
  Devise some rule so I make a difference.

Bucket List

Find the value.
Work backwards,
         and forwards,
Pursue tangents
         and follow them back to the point.
Rising and declining,
Dining and relaxing,
Work. Work it out.
Earn your grade, your degree.
Become a polyglot in self-forgiveness.
The differences between become
         small and smaller as we approach infinity.

This year I will . . .

spoon from the ESSER funds each hour I tutor,
explain the why of $y=mx+b$,
integrate with u-substitution
        or fill in for missing teachers,
bust vapers in the bathroom,
work literal equations
            and maybe wonders,
figure the balance between expectations
                        and grace.

Domain

Forget range,
for now,
as anymore, situations
only go sideways.

This U That

She makes potluck pleasantries:

"What do you do?"

> *I work at the high school,* I say. *An extra body in the math classes, sitting in graffitied desks with the students, modeling how to take notes and pay attention. I'm right there, to encourage them to ask questions, give extra help. Sometimes I "Vanna"—work the problems on the board as the teacher talks, so he doesn't lose eye-contact with the kids. It's a grant-funded position.*

"Oh."

The parent is confused:

"Why are you calling me?"

> *I'm a part of the Student Success Team,* I say. *I can set up a one-on-one meet with your child while they're on quarantine to help them complete their math assignments. They can share their screen and I can walk them through each problem. Have them email me a time and I'll send a link.*

"Ok."

The mid-year hire is curious:

"What, exactly, is your role here?"

> *I am the chewed up piece of gum,* I say, *trod into the floorboards so the kids don't fall through the cracks.*

"Uh . . ."

My nephew snuggles into my lap:

"What is your job?"

> *I'm a tutor,* I say. *You know how your kindergarten class has an extra adult to help out? I'm like that person, except at a high school.*

"So, you go to the high school and toot?"

Order of Operations

Sniffle
Cough
Test
Fatigue
Around here we say *asmotherin'*
when we talk to the doctor.
Then say nothing around
the ventilator,
but pray.

Scaffolding

We thought these were the days
to come, unprepared
as we were,
though they keep coming:
Low tide today was yesterday's high,
the waves increasing in amplitude
as though the full moon refused to wane,
would, rather, spiral in to meet the sea.

The teachers lament,
Why is this year the hardest yet?

Rights County Appalachia

Here, our elementary children
are accustomed to the sound:
semi-automatic pops that ricochet
off the mountainsides
across the screams of their recess play.
They've learned to disregard
the staccato echo.
It's just target practice.

Property Management

What lives rent-free in your heads
that you cannot evict to let new tenants in . . .
How to get you to understand that to solve
$I = b^2 - r$
for b,
I can't get rid of any of the variables in your lives:
       the alcoholic parent
       what that girl put on her story about you
       an empty fridge
       an accidental addiction
       the internal voices begging the body to be cut . . .
Literally, I just want you to
isolate my voice,
shove all that aside for a moment—
       just a moment.
Let me teach you something
complicated, but innocent.
Let me hold you away from your trouble.

Put. Them. Away.

The vacuous hole in
their knowledge
is the exact size
of a smartphone.

Constant

The only constant is change.

In any function, the constant is the number
hanging out alone, no variable at its side.
It is what it is.
Until calculus, when C becomes fixed but unknown.

The coach's wife says to him,
"Nothing changes if nothing changes."
He says nothing, but nods.

Always plot time on the x-axis:
It's the independent variable, always marching on.
Until it isn't.
Like the shortest distant between two points is a straight line.
Except it might not be.

I remember the non-trad who thought she could effectively argue
against non-Euclidian geometry to my old math professor,
both of whom then were younger than me now.

How flat our first knowledge becomes.

My future-physics-professor daughter
returns from the equator where she learned the Pachamama hug:
a spiral, like how they see time:
each moment a chord with harmonics of past and future.
What did they learn, so close to the sun,
watching the stars,
which is seeing time . . .

We learn orbits, as if the sun didn't also fly.
The helix of our DNA, more akin
to our planets' corkscrew through the dark.

I stare at images from the newest telescopes at the planetarium
in my Appalachian Mountains:
lost and dizzy trying to fathom the immense void.
Alone in the universe is really
alone in time.

And what of the twins:
One went to space,
traveled so fast he became measurably younger.
Surely that plot twist shows on a graph,
crumpled into a ball, tossed in a trash can,
so he could keep his birthright.

How precious this tiny world we burn. A magi's gift:
watch chain and tortoise shell become slag and ash.
For what purpose, this rain of myrrh?

x^2 vs. x_2

Superscript:
   the little number (up and to the right)
   has power.
Subscript:
   the little number (down and to the right)
   shows identity
   (which y pairs with which particular x).

Technically, what is the term,
when so many teachers are out
that I serially sub for a sub . . .

I greet the principal each morning
as though he had existential answers:
"Who am I today?"

Apostrophes

Prime—I am past it.
      Knock that exponent pi-in-the-sky
      down a peg—
      I am grey at the first roots.

Double Prime—a shadow
      of my former edges
      ground down—
      any way you factor it
      at this point, I am over the hill,
      my functions decreasing and concave downward.

Teaching on a Full Moon Friday

I don all my talismans:
>   a silver ring from my daughter,
>   a pendant of pressed flowers about my neck.

I shrug into a sweater
>   my grandmother knit my father,
inhale a cloud called rosemary and mint,
intone the spell of my mother's church:
>>   *Peace before me,*
>>   *Peace behind me,*
>>   *Peace under my feet . . .*

A bell to begin and end my meditation.

Mathematics of Change

Often there are infinitesimal changes
in motherhood's demands—
and sometimes leaps:
       twins,
       kindergarten,
       driver's permits.
Now I calculate what
I'm already too late to do:
       on the edge of my family unit's circle—
       the empty nest.

Tea Cup

The missing chip is gone,
   too tiny to glue back anyway.
The roughness mars the brim;
   gone forever the pleasure of the lip
   on a smooth edge.

But to toss it, a greater loss;
   the memory of a gift given gone.

It still holds hot water;
   the handle, sturdy.

Loose leaves of equations for a coaster,
I settle at the table to examine where I went wrong;
work out corrections to turn in tomorrow,
graced with wrinkled rings.

Parallel

I know that glassy-eyed, middle-
distant stare—
   no name on the blank page,
   the problem not transcribed.

All is twisting whisps of fog
so thick we cannot think
who might hear our whimper for direction:
   Morgan le Fey across the misty tarn?
   Marie Laveau in the moss draped bayou?
   Even Marie Curie's ethereal glow is too far away
      to make out the first step.

Any lightbulb over our heads
bounces back an illuminated ignorance.

ΔMath

the trouble lies in the pattern:
   if asked for an answer
   I believe I've been taught
   the ability to provide one

if not, reread my notes,
click the button to see an example,
expand the view of a video explaining how

yet, real life application is
the storied problem—

I chase a green checkmark
in my upper right-hand field of vision—
instant assurance I've made the next right step

as though I could know,
but no, so
                change my grumblings to prayer:
                   work through me
                   the miracles due these students

Sound Decisions

In the constant broadcast of parental
      warnings, worry, advice,
my children seem to have nestled comfortably
      in the dead spots.

Shirking Duties

O, that parents
would function
in their roles

since I could stand to see some
deferential attitudes
toward teachers.

Toss the ball in a parabolic curve
to land in our laps?
As though we were sitting.

Morale Decay

A principal hears
every argument—
every base and petty complaint
in exponential decibels and sullen silence.
They fall into a natural rhythm—
compounded daily, annually—
the background throb of a headache
hidden behind a straight face.
An average agenda may range from
She was looking at me cross-eyed to
He was sawing logs in class.

Vortex

This class period
I am approaching my limits
with the attention-seeking black hole of a human,
who, by my calculations, and
a leap of sympathy,
is likely trying to break
the gravity of trauma.

Feel Attacked

Days come when,
in the precaffeinated
quiet of the morning,
women breathe a revelation—
they are profits.

I am Everywoman.
My struggles are every woman's,
yet uniquely my own.

I should tell someone, they think,
People need to know how important I am.
Ergo, when they agree, indeed,
I will know I am.

Their bones sing with connection
for their weariness has stripped them.
So they rise to inspire
other women wrangling slippery children
and tangled laundry with their own
precious tangled children
and slippery slopes.
They flock to TikTok, Insta, and MeMeMeTube,
a cacophony of borrowed sounds that teach
ADHD by way of FOMO,
and disgorge a false narrative so
their fiction is reflected back to them.

You. You are the noise, O Sisters,
perverting the peace.
Who gets paid for what is sold?
Have you gained the whole world
for your lost souls?

More than the Sum of its Politics

Sometimes limits don't exist
but inflamed, multiplied, conflated
they do, but only if you
come at them from the left
and come at them from the right
and they see each other as equals.

When dyslexics learn trigonometry . . .

compose a trio of chords to sing
　aaahhh
a heavenly sign
like rays of buttery sunlight
melting right through clouds of confusion

fold your feathered wings close
adjacent your body

use your softest voice to say
　fear not

New Math

We return to the basics:
      Breathe in for a count of 4.
      Breathe out for longer, say 5 or 6.
      Again.
      Slow down.
      Signal with your breath for the body to relax.

Melt your forehead.
Soften your jaw.
Smooth down your shoulders.
You are OK. Even if you're not.

We speak aloud
      5 things we can see
      4 textures or temperatures against our skin
      3 sounds we hear
      2 scents in the air
      1 flavor our tongues can find
to step down anxiety,
put us back in our bodies.

We list three people or circumstances we're grateful for:
just little things if we must—
the sun shining, a cat, tater tots for lunch.

We identify two recent times we felt proud of ourselves.

We decorate one happy memory
with additional details—
create a touchstone,
a core recollection to find ourselves
when we get lost in the weeds.

We focus on circles—
what is within our control,
and what we must let go.

We check in with the counselors.
We check in on the counselors.

Some days we work with the lights off
as though so simple a choice could make it *less school*.

Some days we break the rules
and hold each other
through tears,
promise,
You are not alone.

No One Really Understands Gravity

for Julius

The plot holds
no box,
simply a shroud
wound around him, flowers
    scattered
over the mound of earth.

None of us interpreted
the data set,
designed the oscillating regression
to predict such an outcome.

Our thoughts spiral like arms
in the star sea
caught close and far by
the barycenter.

No one really understands
gravity—save mothers—
with voids so heavy
they buckle our knees.

Z-Score of Zero

It is normal
from this vantage point
to look back, not with regret, but
to evaluate how much I may have deviated
from my dreams—the standards I set for myself—
so I might stop on the way back down at those lookouts
I missed on my short-sighted climb. I mean to lengthen
my hiking poles here, walk this gradual decline
with measured intention, find continued
purpose to rise each morning other
than the green-eyed cat's
insistent mew.

$(f \circ g)\ (x)$ or love poem

send me your star charts
graphs of a treasure map
so I can trace
my finger along the curves

we rarely get out of a relationship
precisely what we put in

but I'd even take the time
solve our riddle algebraically
plug away
step after careful step
past all the exes
to find where you've hidden your heart

Abigail 1/700

after Leonard Cohen

The notes she took on the secant chord
while David slept and softly snored
revealed their circumspective meanings to her.
So despite her anxious testing nerves,
the minor arcs and the major curves,
she broke a helpless cycle: Hallelujah.

On the Regular

How many times
are we given practice problems
and we cheat, skip the process
for the appearance of having
our shit together . . .
Plot those along the x-axis
        and watch it all slip away.
                We have no interest in effort.
To the letter, we follow the law of diminishing returns.
They know not to *teach to the test*,
        motivate by fear,
                but they do.

For that final exam on the horizon,
will it even matter if we don't
live in the garden of now
attending the perfection of each and every weed.

irrationals

the reason for the rage
is not imagined, but real
and just because it's not understood
doesn't make it complex

smile
  don't make a scene
    be nice about slights
naturally builds up over time
says
  know your place
slick as oil or *bless her heart*

we want it to end
period
but it keeps on

outlier

with gratitude for Julian of Norwich

. . . but all shall be well
of a morning when
the dog thumps her thick tail on the kitchen tile,
a greeting, like the first cup of black coffee

and all shall be well
of an afternoon when
in February's chill, green cotyledons
sprout under lights in the laundry room

and all manner of things shall be well
of an evening when
the weather warms, so windows are thrown wide
to the spring peepers' sundown song
borne in on eddies laden with lilac

. . . all shall be well,
and all shall be well,
and all manner of things shall be well

He Leaves Instructions on the Whiteboard:
Systems of Linear Inequalities

Name the problem what it is.

When you approach the question,
it is normal to feel frustrated,
see only the signs
for less or greater than,
above or below,
all the lines that cannot be crossed.
You may see only the points that satisfies one,
but not the other.

My beloved students,
even though it seems a slim fragment,
there exists an infinite number of solutions:
the double-shaded region extends forever.
Pick a point and try it.
Prove it true.

Accomplish this together
or on your own.
Show your work.

Series & Rotations

A broken record.
  A broken record.
      When will we ever use this in real life?

Drop the needle on this blues song:

You cannot use knowledge never learned,
      though it can be used against you.
And in your ignorance
you will depend on the mercies,
            or the lack thereof,
of those calculating their own interests,
who do master numbers—
for math and money are links
in chains of power and oppression.

If things feel unfair, count.

So I tally,
captive
in my hyperbolic spiral.

Slashes upon slashes:
horns, teeth, and claws.

My mind,
an old dry-erase board,
holds ghost images
in defiant silence, no matter
the dutiful custodian's absolutions.

Yoga for the Apathy of Rocks

for the pandemic teachers who endure

Some of us women,
at the end of a long day,
gather on the spacious auditorium stage
in a community of quiet privacy,
a half circle radiating tension
to use our bodies to mend our spirits,
engage our cores to center ourselves.
We work on breath and balance
like an equation;
what we do to one side, is done to the other:
   Thread the right arm through the needle.
   Thread the left arm through the needle.
Here, where we source our stress
   in drawn-up shoulders, clenched jaws, and blinked-back tears,
we also ground our tree poses,
cat-cow our way out from behind the curve of computers,
huff out our held disappointments.
This is about
             me.
This is about
             us,
though we don't dare to *ohm* together
lest we create the magic that heals us,
and freed from the umbilical call to return
like the tides, we cease to break ourselves on this work.

2nd Semester

lift open the new notebook
to a clean layer of crystalline snow

linens are cast to drift down
before smoothed across an empty bed

how quiet the night in snowfall
before you write your name upon the dawn

Thoroughly Reasonable Questions Posed
of the Greek Alphabet

Am I not holy now,
  having analyzed
  a transcendental function?

Are they not saints
  for continuing to teach
  through the pandemic?

Are we not immaculate,
  after self-isolation and
  gallons of sanitizer?

What happens once
  we pass our own
  Ω?

for Aimee

I miss them,
though the ornithologist captures
the murmuration: 10,000 starlings,
20,000 wings swoop and swell,
a force of sinuous smoke
above the field
where our sons played soccer together.
I watch the video over and over,
long after they've flown,
the sound like a cresting wave
as it rolls up the beach and back
across the mountain sky.

Midlife Calculus

Would that I could
measure the volume
of a glass half-full

$$V = \frac{\pi r^2 h}{2}$$

but the h of my being
is an unknowable variable.

Nor can I work backwards
the equation for half-life

$$t_{1/2} = \frac{\ln 2}{\lambda}$$

to account for
the value of one well-lived.

I can hope this crisis
is the midpoint

$$\left(\frac{x_1 + x_2}{2}, \frac{y_1 + y_2}{2} \right)$$

and that I don't outlive
the remembrance of my past
to be caught in a möbius present.

I have learned enough, now,
to measure precisely how much it holds,
the irregular curves—
less the difference of the holes life left—
and yet, my heart is still full.

Relative Extrema

1
—¡Tia!— a girl's voice sings out
over the creak of swings. —¡Mira!—
I brighten and turn;
She means me.

2
"Aunt Britt sounds too harsh,"
I tell my sisters-in-law.
Auntie Britt, I decide,
sounds better: part southern,
                part old-school,
certainly the fun aunt name.
The little nieces and nephews
agree, call me
Auntie Butt.

Extended Family

Where's the chapter on *uncle* derivatives?
They are the ones with the sense of adventure,
Who took me fishing on a Sunday,
Taught me banjo and guitar.
They kicked around the soccer ball,
Never plunked me down at the kitchen table
To do my homework.

Overdue Assignments

When I pull from my pocket the world's tiniest violin to play
"Your Heart Should Bleed for Me," all I can see are the $\int$ – ing
mirrored integral signs reflecting across the y-axis of strings to
remind me: back it up. Screw this tiny thing, dilated several sizes
too small for the sound I long to emit. I need the body of a cello or
a body like the sepia toned photos of bare women sitting with their
backs to the camera, $\int$ – holes symmetrically tattooed on the curves
of their waists to widening hips, their spines upright, holding their
heads up on good shoulders.

I rap my pencil to silence the orchestra tuning up, spin it around
and commence the whispered rhythms of solving problems.

$y = mx+b$ or No Math Class on a January Monday

Isolate the why
and the scope and intersectionality become clear:
The crosshairs show the plots plainly.

It will continue forever in opposing directions, unless
we create peacewise functions—
discontinue a slow descent,
bend back the long arc toward justice.

While love is always unconditional,
the parameters can change to include more input.

We learn to listen anew.

at least means it could be more

a student writes you a thank-you note
(leaves it on your desk to read after they've left)

another writes kindly about you in a college application essay
(bravely shares it with you)

one expresses gratitude for your support on senior night
(didn't warn you it was coming)

they keep stopping by your room to say hi
(long after they've passed your class)

several want pictures with you dressed in their caps and gowns
(they are sweat and tears and smiles)

Dementia Sandwich

She can't seem to follow
      the curve of conversation.
Even the smallest jump from point to point
      sends her mind off on tangents—
An infinity of old memories
      triggered by each second.
Naught can be done, and knowing *why*
      is just a diagnosis. The progress continues,
Cuts across the whole of it:
      there is no solution.

Hope for the Future

In Math I
   —by the end of the year—
through sheer rote repetition:
   practice,
      some more practice,
   quizzes, review,
   tests,
      and test corrections
the notion will finally take root:
      the zeroes
      are the solutions.

The Calculus of Literary Journals

After repeated rejections,
the poet is pleased to discover her new work
is supposed to be derivative.

Same

Who is to say the scientist
is not really a theologian searching for truth
in the story of numbers,
graphs, trials, errors, failure, forgiveness.

She asks questions of creation:
      What splits an atom?
The way he might ponder in his heart
      How do we embrace Eve?

Psalms

The translation turned the function
on its head when
enemies became
the shadow within.

The hurts I hold
in my heart are mine—
of my own making.

Unmoored

It looks like I am gestating again,
but it's an inverse function
as I can measure in months until they leave home,
the umbilicus taut,
like from a spacewalk gone awry:
    It seems like floating
        while we speed toward the edges of the unknown.

Methods

"Can you tell,"
my mother asks,
"I didn't spend enough time
at the ocean as a child?"
She picks up another shell,
a blackened shark's tooth,
a disc of green sea glass.

Waves wash errant steps smooth,
turn over a sparkling new view of keepsakes.
We reach and gather,
drop back into the surf what doesn't suit,
rotate the treasures in our hands
until they are too full to hold more.

Gibbous: not all apparent

My skin turns to paper
in this part of the story.

As though years of absorbing the sun
were thrown in reverse
to flame across my skin
blooming through my sternum,
roiling tendrils shifting across my cheeks—

My greatest source of creation has sung
its last bloody song.

How do we lay to rest
what is still within
when it no longer serves us?

To ask is how we age.

Upper and Lower Bounds

If I were a gambling woman,
I'd say, *Run it twice!*
—this life.

But existence itself is,
Even against all odds,
—a miracle.

Halo

Call the old lady eccentric when
she raises her hands to stay
scything blades
from mowing down dandelions.
Give the bees the first fruits of the season:
Sunny golden discs
given time, also go grey—
spheres of tenuous tangents
waiting to be born aloft
on the breath of a child.

Fata Morgana

Across the ocean, a vision
hovers above the waves
of who I might become—
images flipped, one layered over another.
Science says
thermal inversion, bending light, curvature of earth;
an illusion
who siren-sings, promises
pearls for all these agitations.

Which one will resolve
herself to be?

The slap of waves
against the hull,
still in the doldrums,
rocks me as I ponder—
Should I drift, or plot a course
to follow even under darkened skies,
guided by galaxies wheeling away,
light so slow I'd steer by an unfathomable past,
toward a mirage,
a conjuring,
an eventual me,
only assured to vanish.

Additional Acknowledgments

I recognize that some of these poems may, as the kids say, *trigger* some unpleasant memories or thoughts. If you find yourself contemplating self-harm, I urge you to reach out for help. You may feel alone, but you are not. You can call 988, the Suicide & Crisis Lifeline, or text HOME to 471471 at any time, day or night. You matter.

I am grateful to the students and teachers who have included me in their classes over the last several years. I've learned a great deal from y'all: about mathematics and resiliency.

To my first readers—Alessa, Robyn, and Jesse—*Grazie!* Your encouragement kept me going. Thanks, also, to my creative-accountability partner and dear friend, Alena.

It has been an absolute pleasure to find an editor who can hang out with me in the center of a Venn diagram with two circles labeled "people who like math" and "people who like poetry." Thank you, Chris, for making this collection better, and Kevin, thanks and gratitude to you for believing in me—a belief that existed for over a decade before I finally put a manuscript in front of you.

Finally, thanks to my family, immediate and extended: you inspire me. (I love you very much.)

Britt Kaufman lives and writes in the Appalachian Mountains of Western North Carolina. Her gardens are larger than she can manage, but she enjoys listening to sci-fi audiobooks as she weeds. During the school year, she works as an in-class high school math tutor. *Midlife Calculus* is her first full-length collection of poetry which loosely chronicles the year she took calculus for the first time, at age 47, so she could cross it off her bucket list. Her previous chapbook, *Belonging*, was published by Finishing Line Press (2011). Over the years, her poems have appeared in *Scientific American, Kakalak, J Journal: New Writing on Justice, Redheaded Stepchild, Now & Then, Pinesong,* and *Soft Star Magazine* among others. Both of her stage plays premiered at Parkway Playhouse: *Between the Tackles* (2012), about three men who watch football together, and *An Uncivil Union: The Battle of Burnsville* (2011), a romantic comedy set amidst actual historical events during the Civil War. She is a founding organizer of the Carolina Mountains Literary Festival and continued as a core board member for many years. Discover more about her work at brittkaufmann.com

Printed in the USA
CPSIA information can be obtained
at www.ICGtesting.com
JSHW022337170824
68235JS00003B/11